Praise for *Dreaming of Stones*

"Christine Valters Paintner's poems have both a mystical and an earthy sensibility to them, drawing us to the transcendent as well as the immanent presence of the divine. Her poems, much like her nonfiction writing, offer the reader an experience of retreat and sacred encounter."
—RICHARD ROHR, OFM

"Christine Valters Paintner's poetry is a worthy companion to the prose she has already produced. There, her thoughtful analysis of the foundations of modern society stretch the reader beyond any kind of idolatry of the present. Here, she goes even further in her commitment to wed vision to understanding. In this new work she brings poetic insight to observation. She presents the flash of light, the kernel of truth that goes deeper and more mystically into the heart of the universe than fact and faith can hope to do. She makes a bridge for us between experience and wisdom and in the course of it gives us a veritable holograph of life."
—JOAN CHITTISTER, OSB

"These are poems about things that really matter; the tides of time, the lure of landscape, our links to our forebears, our love of home. Paintner has a musical ear and an artist's craft with colour and texture. The work is lushly sensual in its language, generous in its patient wisdom. *Dreaming of Stones* is a collection you will want to keep near you, as a source of comfort and inspiration. Here, the profound is made warmly accessible; the ordinary made wondrous."
—SUSAN MILLAR DUMARS,
poet, author of *Dreams for Breakfast*, *The God Thing*, and *Bone Fire*

"Before I'd even read this collection, I knew I was going to say about Christine's work that in it the spiritual, the human and the poetic segue, moving subtly in and out of each other in each poem. This is hard to achieve with a light touch—but she does. The sequences unfold like breath, a motif that holds the collection together—as do the weather (the word 'storm' appears in both opening and closing poems), the elements and the natural world too. I found myself immersed in the flow of the poems, and the sprinkling of imagination-catching phrases like 'brawl of light,' until by the end I too was saying 'yes and yes and yes.'"

—ROSELLE ANGWIN,
poet, author of *Bardo, All the Missing Names of Love,* and
A Trick of the Light: Poems from Iona

"As a poet for whom the Celtic Christian path becomes ever more significant, I understand Christine Valters Paintner when she describes the kinship between the paths of the poet and the monk. She writes about our journeying to retrieve a lost intimacy with the world in poems sculpted as though from fine pieces of light: delicate things made beautiful for a road less travelled. Perhaps more than anything I am drawn to poems inspired by the early Celtic saints of Ireland for whom nature and a God-created world were inseparable from faith. Their lives were woven beautifully into and through that creation. The stories they leave behind and the poems that tell them are pieces of wisdom for an age trying to travel too fast and too loudly."

—KENNETH STEVEN,
poet, author of *A Song Among the Stones, Evensong, Salt and Light, Iona, Columba,* and *Coracle*

CHRISTINE VALTERS PAINTNER

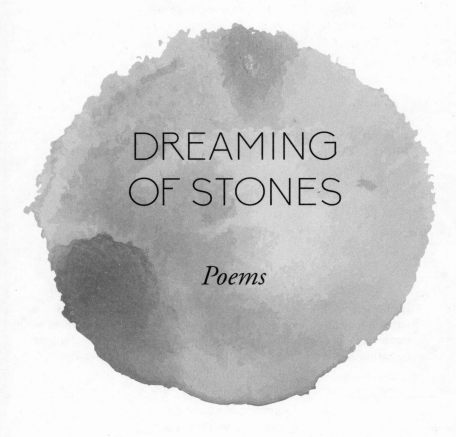

DREAMING
OF STONES

Poems

PARACLETE PRESS
BREWSTER, MASSACHUSETTS

2019 First Printing

Dreaming of Stones: Poems

Copyright © 2019 by Christine Valters Paintner

ISBN 978-1-64060-108-6

The Paraclete Press name and logo (dove on cross) are trademarks of
Paraclete Press, Inc.

Library of Congress Cataloging-in-Publication Data is available.

10 9 8 7 6 5 4 3 2 1

Published by Paraclete Press
Brewster, Massachusetts
www.paracletepress.com

Printed in
Canada

For Kevin and Susan
and the Skylight 47 poets,
with a heart full of gratitude.

———

Paraclete Poetry Series Editor,
Mark S. Burrows

CONTENTS

HOURS

———

THE TIME OF OUR LIVES

———

POSSIBILITIES

———

WILD PLACES

—

LOVE

—

MONKS AND MYSTICS

T he title of this collection, *Dreaming of Stones*, comes from a poem I wrote inspired by St. Ita. She is one of the Irish women saints, and one story about her says she received three stones in a dream. Three is a sacred number in the Celtic imagination. Three moves us past duality into a place of integration, much like poetry can.

Naming the essential "three things" of one's life is a common trope in desert and Celtic traditions. There are a wide variety of responses to that question, which to me indicates there isn't one true answer, but an invitation to consider what is essential in this season of my life now. Poetry works this way as well: what words are essential to the meaning and the music of language? To evoke an experience? Poems help us to uncover this essence, to claim what is essential, to uncover and reveal the wonder already hidden among rock and wildflowers.

Poetry is language carved down to its essence, heightened by rhythm and music, offering a doorway into a new way of seeing, dance between rhythm and image, music and meaning. Poetry brings soulfulness to the world; it amplifies experience, reflecting what is most essential back to us.

"Dreaming of Stones" also refers to my relationship with the landscape in Ireland, where I have now lived since 2012. It wasn't until moving here that I fell in love with the beauty of limestone, granite, marble, and quartz, discovering how each stone has its own textures and qualities, its own stories, and speaks to me of the endurance of landscape and place. "Dreaming of Stones" is about what endures in a world that is fleeting, for example love, imagination, nature, and prayer.

This book is divided into six sections. "Hours" explores the gift of the monastic view of time's daily unfolding, while "The Time of Our Lives" offers poems that explore different and widening rhythms of time. "Possibilities" celebrates the way a poem can crack open a new vision and understanding. "Wild Places" explores the solace and gift of nature. "Love" explores the way of intimacy with the world. And "Monks and Mystics" takes its cue from stories of significant wisdom figures in the Hebrew and Christian traditions. Many of these come from the Irish monks, who have become guides for me in this new home.

I have written many books of nonfiction, but a book of poems offers something different. These poems feel like little love notes to the world, possibilities of seeing things in a new way. I write for those who seek poems rooted in the search for meaning and ancient stories, but who do not want clichés or easy answers.

Making art is an act of community. I write because there are others willing to receive my words, to enter into an exchange of the imagination. I have been offered solace so many times through the poems of another. I also join a lineage of poets, of those who for thousands of years across cultures and language have endeavored to sculpt words and their music to reveal something of life in a new way.

Thank you for joining me in these pages. May these words offer you some solace and inspiration for living well in the world. May you come away seeing things anew.

THIS IS NOT A POEM

but a rain-soaked day keeping me inside
with you and you loving me like a storm.

This is not a poem but a record of a hundred mornings
when the sun lifted above the stone hills outside my window.

This is time for boiling water poured into the chipped cup
holding elderflower, hawthorn, mugwort.

This is not a poem but me standing perfectly still on the edge of the lake
in autumn, watching a hundred starlings like prayer flags fluttering.

This is my face buried in May's first pink peony,
petals just now parting, eyes closed, inhaling.

This is not a poem but the field beyond thought and judgment
and the ways I tear myself apart on too many fine days.

This is the place where clocks no longer matter unless
it is the dusty gold watch which belonged to my grandfather.

This is not a poem but me standing desolate in a parade
of white gravestones, when a single bluebird lands and sings.

This is the bunch of Gerbera daisies you handed to me one foggy
February afternoon, pale yellow like the long-forgotten sun.

This is the first bite of bread after too many hungry days,
this is my grandmother whispering her secrets to me after dusk.

This is not a poem, but me taking off my clothes
and stepping eagerly into the cold mid-December sea.

This is the silence between breaths and in that stillness
this is me saying yes and yes and yes.

HOURS

VIGILS
(for my mother)

Room strung with plastic tubing
like Christmas lights burned out,
fluids delivered and departing
your slack sallow skin,
machine's steady beep
offers consolation for now
in this time outside of time,
while the world beyond the window
bears on with its markets and plans.

I savor these moments
with you still alive, still a promise.
Nurses say you can hear me
so I sing and choke on brine,
trying to seduce you back from the veil.
This waiting is a corridor
with empty dusty chairs,
endless buzz of greenish
lights flickering, moth bodies
frozen behind plastic covers.

On other days I have loved the night
for its dark wisdom and dreams
and lavish gift of rest.
But sitting under this swollen sky,
keeping vigil for the sun
I curse the waiting,
I curse knowing that everyone
I love must one day die.
Wishing for another day with you,
sipping coffee in the morning

together, writing that list
for the store,
buying apples and milk,
making plans
for the weekend ahead.

LAUDS

Lustrous moon lingers
on the western edge of sky
while opposite, the horizon trembles
crimson vines creep up the dome
stars vanish into widening blue hues.

Silence is broken by cries of gulls
awakening to the day as the bright
blaze emerges beyond the sea
my head bows
and my heart cracks open.

LITTLE HOURS

Terce
Morning rush hour, sea of cars swells,
horns and gulls competing.
Third cup of coffee sits half sipped, cold
at my desk and I practice alchemy—
turning words into food and drink for others.
Birds somewhere gather twigs and string
build nests for the season to come,
nightwalkers sleep in caves and dens.

Sext
Flowers stand erect while shadows shorten.
These are the hours too of laundry and dishes,
hotel staff cleaning rooms, excesses of night
vanish under diligent cloths,
earning a wage to buy butter and tulips.
The bay is generous glitter and passersby
rush back from lunch, longing for summer
days to just sit and savor.

None
Quiet sleepiness of afternoon and eyes
turn toward clocks again, counting ticks
to dinner and the latest stories on screens
turn back to complete work at hand.
The dog rests in a triangle of sun
paws twitching with dreams of wide fields.
Attention illuminates corners of the world,
this is the horarium of the ordinary.

VESPERS

The sun slides down
the gap between houses
its amber reach crosses the grass
toward me, shadow of the elder tree
has grown long and I remember
under the mulberry spectacle of sky
how everything I love will end:
this cup of tea with steam ascending,
the dog curled right against me,
your warm hands over mine,
how this sweet leaving of day
makes me draw the world
as close as possible.

COMPLINE

Stars silver
in the violet darkness,
all the midnight wanderers
—cat and wolf, owl and bat—
roam night's trails
ears attuned to another voice.

Step through the doorway
into silence and dream time,
shake off the harsh light of illumination
where the tyranny of answers slips away.
Descend willingly into hush
where you will meet your shadows,
but also your long-hidden
luminous face.

THE TIME
OF OUR LIVES

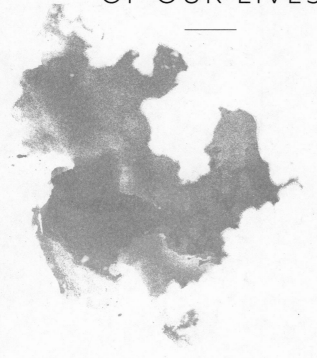

BREATH

This
breathing
in is a miracle,
this breathing out, release,
this breathing in a welcome to
the unseen gifts which sustain me each
moment, this breathing out a sweet sigh,
a bow to my mortality, this breathing in
a holy yes to life, this breathing out
a sacred no to all that causes
me to clench and gasp,
this breathing in is a
revelation, this
breathing out,
freedom.

HOURS

Sit under the long black branches
and await arrival of morning
light when green shoots press
forth, then pink-petaled dawn,
and finally purple weight
of a summer plum at midday
heavy with juice, afternoon
comes and I place an armful
on the table between us,
and we sit silently
by the fire savoring
sweetness well into the night.

SABBATH

Even as the subway car hurtles
into the tunnel and calendars heave
under growing weight of entries,
even under the familiar lament
for more hours to do

a bell rings somewhere
and a man lays down
his hammer, as if to say
the world can build without me,
a woman sets down
her pen as if to say,
the world will carry on
without my words.

The project left undone,
dust on the shelves,
dishes crusted with morning
egg, the vase of drooping
flowers, and so much work
still to complete,

I journey across the long field
where trees cling to the edges
free to not do anything but
stand their ground,
where buttercups
and bluebells sway

and in this taste of paradise
where rest becomes luminous
and play a prayer of gratitude,
even the stones sing
of a different time,
where burden is lifted
and eternity endures.

PHASE

Ivory belly carved
to a sliver and then gone,
three days later, gleam of quartz
appears again among points
of silver fire, circling the sky
slowly like a white cow
in a summer meadow.

The moon is a poem
sometimes full in my mouth
summer's first strawberry
sometimes a communion
wafer dissolving on the tongue
sometimes she is gone
and I gulp at the air
thirsty for darkness.

SEASONS

Spring

Pink, white buds unfold
slowly on black branch tips
quivering at first
then thundering forth in a
riot of color, streamers.

Summer

Nectarine gladness
watermelon slab drips pink
purple peonies
generous summer banquet
how we long to linger here.

Autumn

Pears falling from sky
slush of red, green, and gold
blankets the ground
amber, ruby, citrine leaves
falling, even death is art.

Winter

You can rest now
says the earth, naked branches
tremor in winter's wind
fin and feather fly far off,
warm fur burrowed underground.

LIFE CYCLES

Right now somewhere
someone is being born
skin tender and wet
lung bellows tested
hungry mouth reaches
while choirs of gorse
on the hillside sing.

Someone somewhere right
now is dying, skin slack,
bones press forward,
sister and son bedside
weeping for brevity,
council of trees creak
like an old door closing.

Sometimes the journey between
birth and death is a flash,
mouse fleeting across
the cold floor, cat's hot breath.

Sometimes life is long
a barrel of wine
in the cool cellar
for many summers
until one day
glasses are lifted
and clink,
warmth spreads
through the body slowly
like the lavender dawn.

When I was a child I filled
my pockets with springtime,
daffodils, bits of nest, a robin's egg.

Now I gather my treasures
like dandelion seeds
into my open hands,
close my eyes and blow.

ANCESTRAL TIME

To say their names, an incantation
against loneliness and forgetting:

Suzanne, who fled the suburbs to New York City
birthed one daughter, died too soon

Faith met her love on the Greyhound bus,
fifty years later a slow death from cancer

Marjorie, whose mother died so young
then took passage across the gaping sea

Louisa, divorced 1897, died two years later
records show abuse, desertion

Sarah, a widow, cared for her grandchildren
I wish I knew more

then Sarah again, and back to Mary
whose last name I do not even know

perhaps she is the primordial Mary
maybe Eve is there too.

All that remains now of the motherline,
crumbling papers tracing
births, baptisms, marriages, deaths,
census forms with addresses long demolished,
sometimes a ship's manifest shows
escape or freedom.

What seems so long ago breathes
inside us, we live their lives again,
not understanding the long ache

the need for some primal scream
taking us by surprise one
sunny day, until we hear
all their voices flower in the rage,
and sometimes we hear
their whispers in the night
among shadowed kisses,
how thrusting in the dark
brought forth generations.

They speak to us in dreams,
my body a mirror
and their lives faint fingerprints
seen in the morning light
just upon waking.

COSMOS

That first moment,
explosion of fire and fury
a stampede of suns
light poured into the dark
chalice of space
sparks wheel across
the dome overhead.

We look to the inky sky
to track creatures formed there,
crab and scorpion, lion and bear
stars which died a million years ago
still throbbing with impossible light.

When I close my eyes
I see them still and it seems
they reach to me and I to them.
Is it gravity, or a longing kindled
by stardust within me
or the doorway to forever?

POSSIBILITIES

———

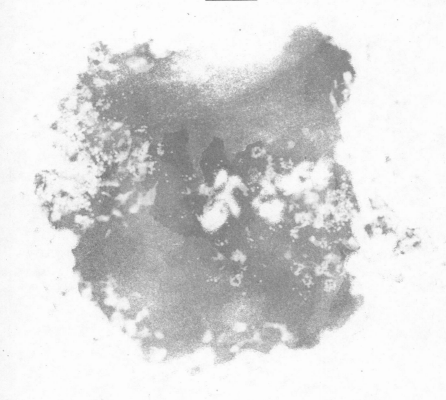

I WANT TO KNOW

I want to sit among trees
and hear the secrets
they whisper in the rustling darkness
to one another,
how they tower so tall
while the world unravels,
roots deep in loam
branches erecting the tent of sky.
I want to know myself
as both earth and heaven.

I want to go down to the shore
on a sunlit October evening
water's cold tongue
edging across land,
a flotilla of minnow
swim by with purpose
and sun suspended
above the horizon.
I want to know my life as both
flame and distance.

I want to climb the mountain
even as bombs drop over faraway places
for here the crow soars above,
even as a gun is fired on a lonely street
a dandelion shoots up now
through granite cracks,
I want to hear the stones
tell their stories of endurance.
I want to know how it is
that they can bear to live forever.

PENDULUM

A silver coin sails across
the black sky making everyone
who sees it rich.

I know too what it is to feel
my poverty when the bowl
of night rolls down over me
with its ceramic thunk.

Some days I am swollen with
possibility, a ripe peach,
fingers sticky with sweetness,
while others I am hollowed out,
a bone scraped clean,
gleaming under the
weight of midday sun.

Many evenings my dreams
extend only as far as the garden gate,
desperate to unlatch the
red and rusted hook,

while others I throw away
the compass and cast myself
into sleep's blue boat and
see where I wash ashore.

RIPE

Summoned by purple
ecstasy of wisteria
and the soft persimmon sun,
I walk down to the orchard,

Did you know a pear tree
is a paradise of limbs and leaves?
Anjou, Bartlett, and Bosc garlands
hang heavy across this palace of light.

Don't pluck too soon, piercing
skin not ready to yield.
Don't wait until they plunge to the
ground in the slush of regret.

The moment is always now,
laden with sweetness of
labor, sunlight, storms,
and a cavalcade of scent.

Eden's slow unfolding
asks me to set aside
my rushed and useful life,
to know myself as ripening.

Does anyone speak the language
of Plum or Pomegranate anymore?
Does anyone hear the quiet
spectacle of blossoms announcing
themselves one by one?

LET IT BE WINTER STILL

Let it be winter a while longer,
let the dark Hours be my closest companion.

Let the owl cry softly
among blackthorn branches,
under the bone sliver
marching upwards across the cold night sky.

Let my heart break for the dead
arriving in boats of misplaced hope
on foreign shores.

Let me shed tears for widows and widowers
in the faraway places we bomb who must
walk through each long day without the
warm calloused hand of their one true love.

Let me weep for the man dying less than a mile away,
alone as he reaches for that bright doorway.

Let me feel the gnawing sorrow of the woman
pressing her hungry children close against her body.

Let winter stay a while longer.

Let me be carried across the haunting threshold
to the places of my own great losses,
until I know this black frozen landscape as my own,
until the mournful songs of my ancestors

fill the air I breathe
until names are etched on my tongue:
Dung. Flood. Hunger.

Let winter linger until I see each naked tree
as a talisman of my sorrow.

Let it be winter until the moment the hour of Spring
breaks through in laboring, gasping, heaving pains.
Until tiny buds burst forth
each one carrying a name:
Crocus. Snowdrop. Peony.

Let it be winter still.

AN UNQUIET REVOLUTION

An uprising of sparrows still sings
the sky awake each morning
and an insurgency of trees insists
on sending forth pink battalions every spring.

The shop clerk wakes early to write a poem,
the man in his suit and tie pauses on the rush
to work as a rumpus of cooing pigeons
puff their gray-black feathers.

A riot of dandelions breaks free of concrete
confines and the exuberance of the dog
at your nightly homecoming is enough to help
you forget what you didn't want to remember.

Corner pub conversation slowly turns
to the brash optimism of planning for tomorrow,
and even though the moon disappears each month,
slowly a brawl of light emerges again.

The earth has moved through another
revolution; there are still many fine mornings
when you just might believe
that anything at all is possible.

IN PRAISE OF FORGETTING

The years heave forward,
an eager puppy ready to play.
I realize I have forgotten
to care about others' opinions,
no longer try to squeeze
into their small minds.

My face decorated with tributaries
Now, my hair
the color of ash,
but gone are the sleepless
nights keeping vigil
for possible catastrophes.

The hourglass nears empty,
I have forgotten even
the ways you turned from me,
seeing your back recede,
a dandelion seed
on a windy afternoon.

There are just a few things
I want to remember:
the wonder that there is anything,
much less bluebells and fresh bread,
the way worlds are encapsulated
in drops of dew.

Let these become part of me,
like breathing and feasting,
a tide or hurricane rising,
and me at their center,
not remembering where they begin
and I end.

"THE DUTY OF DELIGHT"
(after Dorothy Day and John Ruskin)

This poem is held together by heartache,
by the sour smell of sorrow hovering,
thick dust and thinned soup,
the old pillowcase keening-damp,
the swift armada of black clouds.

Even while I write this,
bodies are burned alive in cages,
put on view for the world to see,
bodies are piled in unmarked pits,
or broken by a terrible hunger.

How to remember even the possibility of delight
late one evening after hours of bagging groceries,
the baby crying now, electricity shuts off.
Someone, somewhere, is shredded
and scattered by secret wounds.

Perhaps this is life's most exalted and exacting task,
holding the hard edges against the soft wonder,
or seeking the consolation of nature's indifference.
Even the flame turns to ash,
even the ash is fodder for roses.

What can I do but gather constellations into my arms
like sprays of Queen Anne's Lace?
What can I do but track a creature untamed,
deep into the thick forest?
What can I do but slip open the rusty, lichened gate?

What can I do but read poems before breakfast,
and allow my walking to become a fanfare?
My heart beats like a frog on a hot August night,
while the river rushes past like a herd of wild horses,
and I fall off the ragged edges of the map of known things.

This poem is held together by joy,
even when standing still
we are always rushing east toward the night,
hopeful to meet the sun again soon
soaring in pink perfection.

CUP

Mouth round and strong
walls sturdy,
handle to grip,
tiny chip on the lip,
I pour in cream
making a Milky Way
as it meets
the dark universe
of coffee,
creating galaxies
each morning,
steam breaks through
the cold kitchen air
rising as if to say
"I am here,"
sip, savor, swallow, repeat,
moves over the tongue
down the throat
this doorway to awakening,
cup, bowl, basin, bath.
Our lives are filled with vessels
that save us each day.

"WHOSE SILENCE ARE YOU?"
(after Thomas Merton)

The single eye of the sun long shut,
world deep asleep like a sunken ship loaded with treasures,
full moon's fierce shadows illumine the way for miles,
stars glint like coins dropped to the well's black bottom,
last apple fallen from the tree
in a slush of honey and crimson.

I walk barefoot across wet grass,
night's questions relentlessly wrestling
in my mind's knotted weave.
I look for answers written by salmon in the stream,
or a snail's slither of streaming silver.
I prostrate myself at the gnarled foot of the ash tree.

River softly murmurs her secrets.
Then the wind departs, taking words with it.
Hush cracks open, and
only Silence
blankets my moss-covered dreams
under the mute howl of night.

The long slow leaving of voices reveals
the ancient song of repose.
I awaken covered with dew,
stillness shaken by a single robin.
No longer full of my own echoing emptiness,
I am able to hear at last.

HOW TO BE A PILGRIM

Air travel is like
ancient pilgrims walking on their
knees, flight delays and narrow seats
offer their own kind of penance.

You jettison excess baggage,
leaving behind the heavy makeup case,
knowing the rain will
wash you free of artifice.

Books you wanted to carry left too,
no more outside words needed,
then go old beliefs which keep
you taut and twisted inside.

Blistered feet stumble over rocky
fields covered with wildflowers and you
realize this is your life,
full of sharp stones and color.

Red-breasted robins call forth
the song already inside,
a hundred griefs break open under
dark clouds and downpour.

Rise and fall of elation and exhaustion,
the tides a calendar of unfolding,
a bright star rises and you remember
a loved one waiting miles away.

A new hunger is kindled by the sight of
cows nursing calves in a field,
spying a spotted pony, you forget
the weight and seriousness of things.

Salmon swim across the Atlantic,
up the River Corrib's rapids to the
wide lake, and you wonder if you have
also been called here for death and birth.

This is why we journey:
to retrieve our lost intimacy with the world,
every creature a herald of poems
that sleep in streams and stones.

"Missing you" scrawled on a postcard sent home,
but you don't follow with
"wish you were here."
This is a voyage best made alone.

ASE CAN I HAVE A GOD

Selima Hill)

fossilized, hardened, stiff, unshaken,
not contained in creeds and testimonies,
judgments and stone tablets,
but in the wound breaking open.

Please can I have a God
who asks me to worship at the altar of mystery,
to lay aside certainty, and curl up
in the hollow of a great stone down by the river,
to hear the force of it rushing past.

Please can I have a God
with questions rather than answers,
who is not Rock or Fortress or Father,
but sashays, swerves, ripens, rages
at the rape of the earth.

Please can I have a God
whose voice is the sound of a girl, long silent from abuse,
now speaking her first word,
who is not sweetness or light, but the fierce sound of
"no" in all the places where love has been extinguished.

Please can I have a God
the color of doubt, the shape of uncertainty
who sees that within me dwells a multitude,
grief and joy, envy and generosity, rage and raucousness,
and anoints every last part.

Please can I have a God
who rolls her eyes with me at platitudes and pronouncements
and walks by my side in the early morning
across the wet field, together bare-footed and broken-hearted,
who is both mud and dew.

Please can I have a God
who is the vast indifference of forest and night sky,
who is both eclipse and radiance, silence and scream,
who is everything slow and dark and moist,
who is not measured, controlled, but ecstatic and dancing.

Please can I have a God
who is not the flame, but the flickering,
not bread, but the chewing and swallowing,
not Lover and Beloved, but the making love,
not the dog, but the joyful exuberance when I come home.

ILLUMINATED

"I pray that the eyes of your heart may be enlightened"
—Ephesians 1:18

The window fills with sky
one half pewter,
laden with drops that splash
the cold concrete

the other half brilliant blue
sunlight pours
sidewalk glimmers

in that midday dazzle
you feel like it could
be the first day of creation
or the last
and you know this moment
will not persist

you know you will forget
later in the drudgery
of evening, but for now

you remember how
rain and sun
conspire to show
you everything you need
to carry on to the end of day.

CUCKOO CLOCK

Seconds tick, wooden doors
fling open, tiny carved bird
announces another quarter hour,

each night my grandfather's
heavy feet plod up the stairs,
he pulls the chains downward,

this nightly ritual an act of faith,
hoping to wind it again
on many long nights.

GARDEN FURNITURE

Chaise lounge on wet grass
in her grandmother's backyard,
steel frame rusting, webbing frayed,
she runs outside, rubber thongs smack
her feet like wet kisses,
closes her eyes under
a summer sky full of blue
and sprinklers spilling rainbows,
yet wishes she were elsewhere
rather than those Boston suburbs,
pretends everything about her life
was otherwise.

THE TURNING

Spring shifts to summer,
air fresh like a cucumber,
I drop my heavy bag
and kick off my boots,
skin pressed into sand
and somewhere nearby
the cuckoo announces her return.

INVENTORY
(after Anne Boyer)

I am not writing travel tips, self-help books, or pamphlets that sit
    dusty in waiting rooms

I am not writing postcards, much as I like to receive them, or love
    sonnets, or reviews on Yelp for that French restaurant I adore

I am not writing wedding invitations, thank you cards, or a journal
    filled with my anxieties

I am not writing the ingredient list on the back of a cereal box or
    instructions on a shampoo bottle, lather, rinse, repeat, nor the
    warning sign on the storage boxes that babies might suffocate if
    left to play inside

I am not writing another thesis or dissertation, thank goodness,
    nor am I channeling my grandfather's most intimate thoughts
    through the pen

I am not writing a menu for a five-course dinner with wine pairing
    or the application for a license for the dog who just walked into
    our lives

I am not writing the ten-page leaflet of side effects that comes each
    time I refill my prescription bottle, or my name on a matchbook
    cover

I am not writing a newspaper article or a grocery list, even though
    my fridge is empty

I am not writing a cookbook full of family recipes handed down
    from my Austrian grandmother or what I want others to say at
    my eulogy, not just yet

I am not writing about how my mother's death was my greatest loss
    and how I think of her most mornings still

I am not writing about the way you smile when I become so
    absorbed in putting words to paper that I forget to eat or look
    up when you enter the room.

WONDER

Each day the clock alarms me
coffee aims to undo another restless sleep
and I wonder if the world is
just cup, soap, scarf, and bed?

On some mornings I can see the cup
as chalice, each bar of soap a promise,
the scarf you gifted me, a reminder I am loved,
and the bed a nightly invitation to descent.

Perhaps upon waking
I'll remember a piece of a dream,
just a glimpse of a yellow balloon
that lifts me into the wide sky.

WINGS

I wake from a dream,
reach toward day as it hatches,
its tiny beak presses against
the delicate shell of sky.
Today I might learn to fly.

WILD PLACES

WILD

The night I was born
a riot of starlight broke out,
moonlight a ripple of egret's wings,
constellation Lupus howled
and Ursa Minor growled
to welcome the arrival of animal being.

The sun trapezes ten thousand times
across the pale blue sky,
while I learn manners and
the rigid confines of politeness,
learn to speak quietly and hold back.

Magpies soar overhead,
igniting a dim memory
that I was once like this,
feathered muscles rising and falling,
grateful for horizon and emptiness.

Or standing by the sea's roar,
I long to rush out
into the wild waves,
to see where I would be washed ashore
or if I might finally grow fins.

When the end of my life arrives
I want you to be able to say
late one evening you saw me draped
in fireglow and could just
make out my whiskers quivering.

That you couldn't see my fur in night's embrace,
but you heard it brushing against
the needles of Scots pine,
my dark eyes scanning the forest,
seeking to return home again.

THRESHOLD

You find a place to sit,
spine cradled by hazel branches
and finally rest arrives.
The grief you didn't even know was there
breaks the banks within, so carefully built,
and you discover a river inside you.

Then follows the sweet stillness
when you gather your strength for what is still to come
when you eat your cheese sandwich on brown bread,
prepared early this morning,
long before you knew how your life
might break open in a flash,

the way the breeze
catches dandelion seeds
and suddenly there is just stem
and a shower of shooting stars
and time as your only companion
to wait for what is to come.

You begin to walk and your sweater
catches on hawthorn branches,
you think of a little breathless girl
running through a fairy tale forest,
except you are no longer running away,
but headlong into the council of trees,

and you know this moment as a new beginning
with no idea of what is arriving,
only for the sudden departure
of the burden you have been carrying for a lifetime,
leaving instead an unfamiliar lightness
as you struggle not to ascend toward the sun.

How you no longer need
to carry this heavy stone in your arms,
on your back, in your throat,
and you wonder why you didn't lay it aside long ago
and you see how your curled fingers
have become frozen in their grasp.

The grass suddenly is
more vibrant than you ever remembered
and you are free to gather an armful of wildflowers,
gentians with their bowls of sky,
buttercup mouths full of sunlight,
constellations of Queen Anne's lace.

Bees are thick with nectar,
and even the stones sing on this wet morning
where limestone hills stretch gray into the steel sky
their chorus lingering in the distance
and as the rain falls,
baptism doesn't feel so very far away.

CONNEMARA ILLUMINATED

A poem is being scribed this morning
across the thick brown bog and
over the gashed granite folds of mountain,
written in spires of gold descending
from the wide bowl of sky
across the breathing heather.

You have to pause to read it,
long enough to hear beneath the relentless
moan of wind
where centuries of voices have whispered
their seeking, feasting, fasting, loving.

You know your singular aloneness
and your place in a communion of stone and sea.

Even as the kestrel's wings vibrate into the night
sending quills into the damp air,
even as the skylarks and stonechats
attend each day's awakening
like eager midwives,
this empire of longing writes its script
in fox tracks and memory.

If your life could be just a fraction of this poem
you would never need to utter another word.

TREE DREAMING

I swallowed a seed last night
and dreamed I planted myself
in a sea of loam sometime
before the periwinkle dawn.

The awful ecstasy of
cracking open,
stretched taut between
dark earth embrace and
a crown of stars circling.

Time no longer measured
in clock ticks but by arrival
of a glut of blossoms,
plump fruit hanging low,

followed by death's jeweled spectacle,
wind-ravished,
branches naked,
shadowed silhouette
in the feeble winter sun.

Let me linger here with delights
of the gray squirrel's
soft burrowing into my body,
all breath and fur,
a murmuration of starlings
filling my limbs with music,
chorus of wild irises' golden
tongues wagging at my feet,
or the pleasures
of being rain-soaked
on a summer afternoon.

Let me sleep
a while longer.

I HAVE ALWAYS LOVED THE SEA

Late June,
curtains opening like a sail,
splashes of sunlight
dazzle me awake.

Beyond my plans
for how to spend the day,
I hear the great breathing
of the sea.

A barefoot walk to the shoreline,
past violet mussels and
hardened moons, ripples
of bladderwrack and dillisk.

My arms and legs now coated
with blue-gray scales
gills wide open to
gulp down salted air.

All the rivers have been
called here too,
to empty themselves of ideas,
to learn the ocean's fluency.

There is a great tide within me,
already rising, always receding.
Despite the sea's indifference,
I feel my exile less keenly here.

I who love the horizon can
finally see beyond seeing,
and I dive beneath
the slate blue surface.

SHADES OF WINTER

This land is not just mineral and bone
but sepia dreams of fox
quivering in warm underearth,
meadow showered with pale lemon light.
Herons swim quietly across a steel sky.
Starlings swivel above the lake,
their inky dance penning a confession.
A river whispers among alder and pine
shouts her white surrender to the sea.
Silk threads sewn into the hem
of shoreline unravel in strands
of dillisk and purple bladderwrack.
The milk glass moon ascends
through blue silence, and if the heart
has not yet come undone,
a pink blossom pressed
in the pages of a summer book,
is blown aloft by winter's gusts,
and there, among the heather,
is set free.

MOUNTAIN PRESENCE

Gorse blooms early this year
a golden ring
around the hem of the mountains'
long brown skirts.

I envy their granite endurance
through a million cycles of flowering
and falling, witness to hunger and war
yet standing ever so still.

I hold out my finger
and trace the great folds
of their generous bodies,
goddesses each and every one,

or a herd of sleeping elephants
lying shoulder to shoulder
and I wonder what it will take
to rouse them?

To say their names
is almost an incantation:
Mweelrae, Lackavrae, Binn Mhor,
Letterbreckaun, Derryclare, Bencor.

So often these dark days I grow weary
and want to climb one slowly
and hear how silent it is,
how the naked bog draped in heather

gently breathes, and I want to lie down
on the pinnacle and dream
of stars and comets,
feel the earth's longing to kiss the sky.

Every palette feels muted now,
and then morning rays arrive at an angle,
pour down across barren hills
and suddenly there is color and light
and suddenly everything seems possible again,
dillisk dances in the brine nearby
a crow swoops wildly
and I know something of me might also endure.

WINTER SEA

Slate gray waves crawl up the sand
scent of seaweed and salt
clouds part and silver light dazzles
for a moment before rain reappears.

My hood pulled close over my ears
flapping fiercely in frozen wind
gulls swoop, shriek, and soar,
tide reveals all that has been hidden.

I step across large smooth stones,
full moons each of them
dillisk splayed on sand, ink drawings,
no other person here.

THIRTEEN WAYS TO LOVE THE RAIN

(after Wallace Stevens)

I

Moss profusion dangling from branches

II

bucketing, lashing, mizzling, a whole vocabulary

III

sun's glimmer on wet stones

IV

the way a broken umbrella dances, urban tumbleweed

V

walking home that night so soaked I no longer cared

VI

moodiness of rain, defying perpetual optimism

VII

splashing puddles in wellies, like we did as children

VIII

curling up to read by rain-splattered windows

IX

fat drops falling slowly, then gaining momentum

X

the ferocity of storms, wind blowing you sideways

XI

arcs of color crossing the sky

XII

birds huddled on quiet city streets,

XIII

how it keeps me inside with you.

SHORELINE TRIPTYCH

Foam crawls on its knees,
then retreats, this is me
on finer days trying
to reach toward
something solid then falling
back and reaching again.

Jellyfish drift and sway,
translucent globes
sting when you come close,
I wonder if sometimes
I reveal too much
then lash out as you approach.

I lie here counting
an eternity of shells,
remnants of another life,
spirals pointing
inward and outward
all at once.

NEW BEGINNINGS

Dandelions, daisies, and buttercups
wave in the wind their yellow hello,
green hips sway the hula.

If I listen closely I hear them
ask me to say yes too,
to let loose my petals,

be buffeted by breezes,
step through the doorway
beyond the clock's tick.

Bog cotton clouds drift
east now in the direction
of dawn.

PIGEON OF PATIENCE

Each morning
you perch
outside my window,
look out over
the lake of rooftops
wait, puff, coo,
for me to feed you.

Some days I forget,
or rush on, I don't even
like the gray feathers
coated with city grime,
tiny orange eyes, head bobs,
instead I wish for
starlings and sparrows,
but still you return
sometimes with friends,
reminding me of what it is
to hunger and hope
and still I scatter seeds.

TAKE MY HAND

Please don't plant me
neat rows of rosebushes
and tulips at attention,
no manicured gardens
or crystal vases of cut stems.

Instead, take my hand,
lead me onto
rain-softened grass
which undulates like a boat
on a summer lake,

lie down with me
in a quilt of sunlight and shadows
among yellow petals, violet trumpets,
a feast for hares and bees,
let's linger and forget ourselves

until even the tiled sky above
is cracked open by stars
and all that is restless and wild
within us can roam the heavens
howling the moon aloft.

VISITATION FROM FOX

Flash of orange
darts across the street
like an emergency flare,

long snout, triangle ears,
body a field of fur, tail ripples
behind, a party streamer,

disappears into thick thorns
of hedgerow as quickly
as it came.

Keeper of secrets
of forest and underbrush,
how did you know

I needed to remember
how wild things still thrum
beyond the road's edge.

LOVE

———

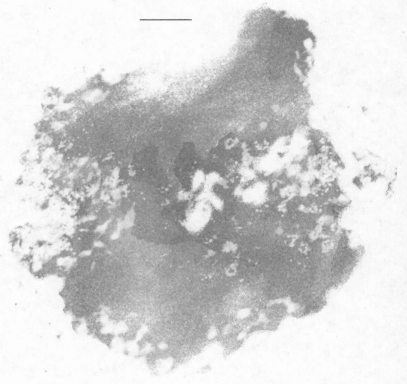

LOVE

Color of amber, life seized inside
taste of summer's first peach
sound of a dog's satisfied grunts
smell of compost, leaves, earth, dust
feels like a winter's day by the fire
with nowhere else to be.

SING

Come sing, I bid you sing
under the trees your song lifts
me like a bird

fly with me
my starling

       and let's sing like we have never sung before
       from the long bare branches just bursting
my heart in bloom,
a shower of pink petals blankets the earth
          die
          or sing

the choice is ours to make – you and me
to sing when rockets launch
to sing when the grave is filled
to dance like
petals
falling

only for me to remember – how to love you
only for me to remember – what the earth desires

come sing or don't sing
under a wide sky with me
breathless.

FINAL INSTRUCTIONS

The palaces you build
are always temporary;
soon the blaze will
burn this spectacle down.

Remember the gifts this fire
once brought, illuminating
landscape on a cold night,
revealing the shape of things.

Follow your longing
to hang upside down in trees,
letting dreams tumble out,
along jumbled alleys of bark and fern.

Let yourself be nourished
by these stark hills
and feel how the lifting tides
elevate something in you.

See the scattering of shells
at your feet, how the gulls'
cries break open
the vault of blue above.

Press close to me now
this chilled night,
our wisps of breath sending
love letters into the air.

Let the celebration continue
under the moon's steep climb,
even while the limestone crumbles

and the last train leaves,
its amber light receding
into the dark.

THIS IS HOW THE WORLD IS SAVED

I stand on the bridge
river rushing beneath my feet
headlong into ocean.
The tide is full and here
under a cold night's sky
I can see my own end so easily
which will come one day regardless.
Why press on under the burden of bills,
each day a new ache,
and the sea's inevitable rising?

I remember you at home waiting for me
to bring the Chinese takeout for dinner,
potstickers, sweet and sour pork, white rice.

I remember the dusty bottle of red wine with the
French words on the label, sitting alone on the counter,
which your mother gave us on her last visit before she died,
to save "for a special occasion, a celebration."

I remember the way your kisses came so freely
when we first met and warmed corners of
me no one else could reach.

I remember the little splash of cream left in the
red plastic container in the fridge,
perfect for a cup of coffee before bed.

I think of how a thousand lives are spared
by wine and kisses and cream every day.

And even though when I get home
the cream has turned
and you have turned from me as well
because dinner has grown cold
and I remember that bridge
again with longing,
but instead

I sit down to the table
and finally open
that bottle of wine
and pour myself a glass.

LAST NIGHT I DREAMT I WAS

spying on the life I thought I wanted,
the grand sweep of space,
flinging myself out to the very edges,
climbing from silver day to flushed evening,
feeling the pulsing stretch of wingspan.

Last night I dreamt I was flying,
slow circles though space,
ascending north to see polar bears
with their curls of breath and then
rainbow ribbons spreading across sky,
stitching stars together.
I swooped and swirled through
orange canyons, over blue peaks,
inhaling the world
like freshly plucked blossoms.

Last night I dreamt I was crying,
unbearable untethered freedom,
seeing my shadow cast far below.
I ached for you out of reach,
I soared expecting a symphony of spheres,
but I just missed your song.

Last night I awakened from a dream
your spine pressed against mine,
the weighted warmth of blankets,
dawn light distilled, summoning forth
the world. I thought of the hedgerows
outside our door heavy with herbs,
and rain murmuring on the grass.

Sometimes I look up and see trails
of myself traversing the sky.
But mostly I am grateful for gravity.
Grateful for all that keeps me in your orbit.

THERE IS NO TIME FOR LOVE TO BE BORN

"Aren't there annunciations / of one sort or another / in most lives?"
—Denise Levertov

There is no time for love to be born
in a world flailing under fear,
trampled by terror, crushed by callousness.
There is no room for love to be born
under the heft of pressing grief,
no open portals in the perpetual busyness
or the list of endless tasks minted newly each morning,
where "to do" never seems to include "love more."
No opening in the jostled and tinseled shops,
which promise to soothe the ache and awfulness of our burdens.

I see you there holding your infant son, pink-scrubbed and new.
I see you there holding his grown dead body, brutalized and hollow.
Your sobs rumble as he is lifted from your arms,
longing to still be earth-tethered by the weight of blood and bones.

You are not orbiting the sun,
but instead the great dirge, swaying me from note to note,
the wailing daughter whose mother's heartbeat has just halted,
the river's cold splash when another one gives up,
the soldier's wound which sends him home,
the slivered crescent descending against a black horizon,
the winter's pale morning light streaming between dusty curtains,
the newly discovered constellation.
You are the birth mother and the death mother.
There is no time for love to be born,
only the willing descent into all the battered and frozen places,
the opening of doors long ago latched and rusted.

You are the breaking open of star-streaked
cracks where woe loses its sturdy grip,
where in the most ordinary of moments,
when all else nudges us further toward despair,

suddenly we feel the wild impulse arising
to say yes.

INHERITANCE

I take down the generic
white jug from the shelf,
the one made with ten thousand
others in a factory in Taiwan.

I wish it were the Meissen porcelain one
with the blue onion pattern that survived
two world wars, but not my need
for funds to finish graduate school.

I long, too, for the cut crystal bowl,
etched with delicate flowers
in which you served ripe, sweet berries
but was later sold to pay for books.

Or the silver set with your initials
engraved on the handles, I imagine
a stranger now running her fingers along
the grooves those letters make.

I only held onto the coffee cups from which
you sipped your *Kaffee* in the afternoons,
a slow pause in the day, your eyes looking
far into the distance.

ELEGY FOR MY MOTHER

Until you died
and I wandered endless hours
among trees stripped bare as I was
I didn't know how much I loved winter,
how the single crow cawing could console,
how sky so wide and dark
offered me respite from the world's
demand for brightness.

Until you died
I didn't know how much gravestones,
so heavy and cold, and those granite angels
could meet the density of my longing,
winged ones weighted down
with their own grief, their loss
of capacity for flight.

Until you died
I never knew how cheerful everyone
tries to be, the forced march of optimism,
when sometimes all that is called for
is tears and crying out long
into the moon-slivered night.

160 EAST 48TH STREET

"(T)he house we were born in is physically inscribed in us."
—Gaston Bachelard, *The Poetics of Space*

Sometimes at night
I am there again.
Midtown Manhattan,
all concrete and spires and sirens,
funneled along stone alleyways
by blinking
red, yellow, green.

Doorman sentry
allows me passage,
witness to arrivals and leavings.
Twelve stories up in the elevator,
that feeling of going aloft
to our home suspended in air,
still carved in me like a whisper.

Our living room, with the
Chrysler building view
vanished on foggy mornings,
and the sea of brick-framed
windows thick with city-grime,
all those lives laboring
ferociously behind them.

There is the dusty metal tray
in the kitchen with half-drunk
bottles of scotch and vodka,
and the smoke rising
in silver curls from the ashtray
there on the plastic-covered table,
the window cracked open.

Fire ambulance wail heralds
some nearby suffering.
A pigeon lands on the sill,
in a world full of clamor
its cooing comes like
a quiet annunciation.

LISTEN

I wake to a rising of robin voices,
their tiny chests puffed like ripe persimmons.
Acres of clouds strum across the day-blue sky,
wind breathes its endless score over heathered hills
and the sea beyond my window churns.

Somewhere a hazelnut drops rustling to the ground.
Peony peels herself open in a slow yawn
to reveal a multitude of pleasures.
Fox darts between hedgerows, breaking her silent reverie,
orange fur brushing against golden gorse profusion.

Beneath sirens and the perpetual groan of cars,
the march of trains and planes propelled by timetables,
beneath the endless clatter of your own mind, you can,
for a moment, hear the asparagus heaving headlong into spring.
My labor is to love this secret symphony.

You curl yourself around me at night,
song of your breath stuns me into the sweetest sleep.
And the blue glass vase sits on the table beside me,
holding roses you bought because they smelled like an aria.
When this is over, all I want to say is that I heard the music
of the very last petal

drop.

REQUIEM FOR MYSELF

When I die
plant a pinwheel
in an open field
where winter's wind
and rain march forcefully
across in battalions,
and you can stumble
out there to meet me
one late afternoon
when you feel the world
must surely be ending.

You, soaked
from tears and storms,
kinship with dark sky.
Me, rainbow axis whirling,
an orbit of
joyful defiance.

You then, inspired,
tumble gleefully
across grass, pirouette,
forgetting for a moment
grief's burden,
knowing the world
will be with you
for many years to come.

Never think
this brief sojourn wasted
as you head back
to the fire waiting at home,
laughing to yourself
the whole way.

BLOODLINES

It had been a season of death.

Our sweet Weimaraner developed dementia,
running herself in circles late at night.
My mother-in-law no longer recognized
anyone, had entered her final season.

I flew to Vienna solo, a pilgrimage
to my father's grave, buried
when his too small heart had given
out so suddenly many years before.

The deep ache in my thigh was the first herald,
making me feel like I also had wrestled
with the angel all night. But having just flown
five thousand miles I dismissed it as aging.

Then came shortness of breath
on my long, lingering sojourns through
the streets of this city I loved, and thought,
surely I am tired from so much travel.

Five days later, in the emergency room.
the young and eager doctor looked at my blue,
swollen vein, and pointed to the wheelchair:
"Don't move a muscle while we run tests,
the blood clot could dislodge and kill you
instantly."

Endless needles and x-rays, blood work,
ultrasound, and finally the CT scan
which several hours later revealed the
offending clots in my lung and leg.

1 in 3 don't survive, I was later told.
My life didn't pass before my eyes.
Instead, I was
frozen in a moment,

haunted by the image
of my body found alone, bundled in a green wool coat,
lifeless in front of the statues of those lions
baring their teeth at passersby.
I imagined the phone call to my husband and
the aching grief that would follow. My first thought:
I hadn't left him enough details
about our bank account passwords.

Some people say God saved me that day,
but I don't care for platitudes. Fierceness
rose up in me; otherwise, it would have been
easier to yield to the dark corridor.

My husband rushed to my side,
like those romantic cinema depictions.
You would think I'd have cleared up
that banking issue first thing,

instead I clasped his hand in mine,
I held his warm, rough skin close, and as
we walked slowly into the winter day together,
I saw the clouds arising from his breath like
incense, an offering.

SLANT

Late October afternoon
when rain briefly lifts
and the light forms a
golden slide from the sky,
so that everything
I have ever longed for
suddenly rushes headlong
into the world.

Trees brilliant in their rust-hued gowns,
leaves flutter like prayer flags
descending to expectant earth.
Hedgehogs curled in their caves,
fox slinks quickly by—an apparition.

You are there too,
just beyond the sheer curtain
you slumped behind all those years ago,
your hollow eyes collecting pools of rain.

Suddenly you rise up, come close,
tell me you know just how hard
I have worked these years
to save you, to get you to turn
your face toward me again.
Riding the wind is a whisper,
You can rest now.

And the sun's slant cracks open
a stony place in me,
and in autumn
a tiny green shoot
pushes through.

IN PRAISE OF CIRCLES

"I live my life in widening rings
which spread out to cover everything."
—Rainer Maria Rilke

Friends around the dinner table
their mouths making o's of delight and laughter,
plates piled with new potatoes, pearl onions, and pork loin.

Time softens the edges of river stones,
the arc of waves reaches for shore,
celestial orbiting spheres keep cosmic time.

There is the saffron yolk, blood oranges and blueberries,
the coins in my purse that let me buy fresh meat and vegetables,
a steaming bowl of bone broth.

St. Hildegard of Bingen saw the universe as a cosmic egg,
and St. Francis of Assisi displayed those wounds in his palms,
icons halo their heads with gold.

The mossy green iris of my lover's eyes, lost together
in a circle of mingled limbs, breasts and bellies, imperfect,
soft, and round. The ring he slid on my finger years ago.

The curve of the old woman's back bent over
from a thousand griefs.
The pregnant belly ripening.

Monks arising for prayers, entering
the great cycle of rising and falling,
Sufi dervishes whirling, always left around the heart.

A circle is both diameter and circumference,
compass and horizon, holding center and edge together,
calling us to the heart and the wild borders.

Winter's fierce stripping away will always come again,
but so will dahlias and desire. Memories unbidden, circle
around like birds returning from migration.

Progress isn't just the steep ascent up the holy mountain,
but the descent back to the daily, those friends still
lingering by the fire, the bottle of wine now lying empty.

CORRIDOR OF GRIEF

You walk down the long dusty hall,
dim lightbulbs dangle,
pictures tilted on the wall
you pass each one and look,
sometimes it is her crooked smile
or him frowning in the sunlight
or a still life with oranges
and you remember the juice down her chin,
and you're choked again by a river rising.

No way of knowing
why you keep walking,
no fabled light beckoning,
just the sense that if you stop
you'll be swallowed
and spit out again,
people pass you by
asking how you are
but don't pause for an answer.

When sleep finally comes
you dream of them –
run your fingers through his hair,
hear her laugh again –
and you long for all the things
that once annoyed you,
the long hairs left in the sink
or the pile of shoes
on the bedroom floor.

MONKS
AND MYSTICS

DREAMING OF STONES

In the world before waking
I meet a winged one,
feathered, untethered,
who presses in my palm
three precious stones,
like St. Ita in her dream,
but similarities end there,
her with saintliness and certainty,
me asking questions in the dark.

All I know is
I am not crafted from
patience of rock or gravity of earth,
nor flow of river,
I am not otter with
her hours devoted to play.
I am none of these.
At least not yet.

The stones will still be singing
centuries from now,
made smooth by
all kinds of weather.
If I strike them together,
they spark and kindle.
Do I store them as treasures
to secretly admire
on storm-soaked days?
Or wear them as an amulet
around my neck?

When the angel returns to me
in the harsh truth of last morning,
will she ask
what have I endured,
treasured, and sparked?
Will she ask what have I hidden away
and what made visible?

HOLY MOUNTAIN

I want to climb the holy mountain
ascend over weight of stone
and force of gravity, follow the
rise of a wide and cracked earth
toward eternal sky,
measured steps across the sharp path,
rest often to catch my heavy breath.

I want to hear the silence of stone and stars,
lie back on granite's steep rise
face to silver sky's glittering points
where I can taste the galaxies
on my tongue, communion of fire,
then stand on the summit and
look out at the laboring world.

I want to witness earth's slow turning
with early light brushing over me,
a hundred hues
of gray, pink, gold,
speckles of Jackson Pollock light,
then ribbons of mist floating
like white streamers of surrender.

I want to look back down the trail
over my past, forgive a thousand tiny
and tremendous transgressions
because now all that matters
is how small I feel under the sky,
even the sparrowhawk takes no notice of me,
how enlarged I feel by knowing this smallness.

I want to be like St. Patrick,
climb the holy mountain full of
promise and direction and knowing,
forty days of fasting aloft among clouds
until my body no longer hungers
and something inside is satisfied
and my restless heart says *here*,
no longer dreaming of other peaks.

ST. GOBNAIT AND THE PLACE OF HER RESURRECTION

On the tiny limestone island
an angel buzzes to Gobnait
in a dream, disrupts her plans,
sends her in search of nine white deer.

She wanders for miles across
sea and land until at last
they appear and rather than
running toward them

she falls gently to wet ground,
sits in silence as light crawls across sky,
lets their long legs approach
and their soft, curious noses surround her.

Breathing slowly, she slides back
onto grass and clover and knows
nothing surpasses this moment,
a heaven of hooves and dew.

Is there a place for each of us,
where we no longer yearn to be elsewhere?
Where our work is to simply soften,
wait, and pay close attention?

She smiles as bees gather eagerly
around her too, wings humming softly
as they collect essence of wildflowers,
transmuting labor into gold.

ST. CIARAN AND THE DREAM

Scent of morning startles and
Ciaran wakes from his dream.
All that lingers is the silvering
river which runs through the fallow field
of his mind, banks swerving around
an opulent oak, brown antiphon of swallows
singing praises, saying *here*.

Hunger of daylight becomes his compass.
Overhead, blue vaults the umber earth
as he follows veins of quartz across granite –
an atlas of the heart –
until he finds the river rushing
and he rests under the glorious tree
and breathes fully and finally free.

ST. COLMAN'S BED

A grief-sparked journey,
you tread porous limestone
past fields of wildflower and rock
finally see the hawthorn tree,
guardian of the place,
who asks you to bend low

through a halo of hazel scrub
to arrive where the well comes
from a fissure in the mountain's rib
and sends forth white scarves
billowing downward past your feet
toward the sea far beyond.

Before you reach your hands into the water,
you climb a bit further to the cave
stand within, stretch your arms out, touch each side,
you think of Colman sleeping there for years
and you wonder if here he could avoid the pain
of the world or did it just echo in rock and flesh.

You imagine his companions here too,
the rooster who woke him at dawn
for prayer, mouse nibbling his ear
when he fell back to sleep,
the fly who sat still for hours
marking his place on parchment.

Perhaps you finally scream and cry and sob,
let loose the sorrow that has burrowed its way
into sinew and tendon, release it into the open mouth
of this dark cavern, hoping Colman
or God or the spirits of this place
might hear you, until there is nothing left,
until you find yourself back at the well again trying
to drink, unable to keep up with the rush of water,
while on the branch of the rag tree overhead,
its wings damp from mist,
its apricot breast full of breath and life
a robin sings of the beauty found in stones and thorns.

FLAGSTONE OF LONELINESS

"Don't fear suffering with all its heaviness,
give it back to the burden of the earth's weight;
heavy are the mountains, heavy the seas."
—Rainer Maria Rilke, *Sonnets to Orpheus*

On nights when my heart is
thick with sadness and my
limbs and sighs are ballast,
I long to lie down on the
flagstone of loneliness
like Columcille before
he sailed to Iona, leaving behind
the land he loved.

What do the stones feel as
they gather our heaviness
into their granite endurance,
so patient as clouds release
their burden of rain upon them?
Even rivers part ways for boulders,
not willing to risk splitting them wide
and unleash the channel of ancient grief.

We climb rocky summits,
under the illusion we can defy
the gravity of sorrow,
hearts pounding in exhilaration
while mountains grow weightier
under tender feet.

If you sit by a stream and listen
as water makes music over rocks,
you will hear them keening.

ST. SOURNEY'S WELL

Gentian blue sky,
dandelion seed clouds play
hide and seek with the sun.

Brightly colored ribbons hang
from hawthorn, old party
streamers from branches, banners

of longing: a prayer for healing
the great divide of the heart,
or a beloved consumed by cancer.

Or simply an echo of the psalmist's
ancient cry, "How long, O God?"
into the vast and thunderous silence.

Walking the rounds, always sunwise,
slowly arriving, footsteps bless
the ground, saying I am here.

No pronouncements in reply,
no choruses of Alleluia.
Only moss and streams and birdsong,

only knowing that life still
burgeons here on the edges of
our own landscapes of loss.

I plunge in my hands.

ST. ENDA ARRIVES ON INISMOR

It must have been the light
slanting across veils of rain,
when this island, all gray stone and bare
became a vision in gold and gleam

or perhaps it was the smell of sea,
wind swirling up the stony spine,
gulls criss-cross, weaving a new story,
one more truly your own

and something in you had already
bowed low, astonished,
you found yourself singing
after so many years of silence

and the great betrayals of your life
sheared away like winter's wool,
a quiet descends on your thoughts
and you know there is no leaving.

Slowly, hundreds follow also seeking
the way light and water and stone
can remind of elemental things,
how time suspends as it travels

out on the tide,
returns with its offering:
your reflection in the pools formed
on shore, you no longer look through but in.

ST. DEARBHLA'S EYES

Fleeing from Meath to Mayo
her betrothed gave chase,
she turned to face him, ask
what he loved about her,
"your eyes" came in ardent reply
so she plucked them out
each a perfect orb
cool in her hands like beads
and in horror he fled.

She stood there smiling
surprising even herself
relief rushed down her limbs,
she bent over the well,
splashed her face
and those hollow sockets
with scent of mineral and moss,
sight restored in a flash.

She looked at the world
as if for the first time,
she could finally see
how her God was always
on the side of freedom,
how everything glistens,

and how we must risk everything,
trust we were meant
for this, as if telling
the truth for the first time,

as if our hearts
had been plucked out too
and set ablaze
for all the world to see.

ST. BRIGID AND THE FRUIT TREE

There was the moment
you could bear it no more.
Your eyes brimming with
glistening drops
summoned by the hunger of
the world, the callous and
terrible things men and
women do to one another.

Your tears splashed onto
cold stony earth, ringing out
like bells calling monks to prayer,
like the river breaking open to
the wide expanse of sea.

From that salt-soaked ground
a fruit tree sprouts and rises.
I imagine pendulous pears,
tears transmuted to sweetness.

There will always be more grief
than we can bear.
There will always be ripe fruitflesh
making your fingers sticky from the juice.

Life is tidal, rising and receding,
its long loneliness, its lush loveliness,
no need to wish for low tide when
the banks are breaking.

The woman in labor straddles the doorway
screaming out your name.
You stand there on the threshold, weeping,

and pear trees still burst into blossom,
their branches hang so heavy, low,
you don't even have to reach.

ST. BRIGID AT THE MARKET

I see her in the market
backlit in the doorway
from the evening sun,
blue cloak ripples like water
dandelions and primrose in her hand.

Passersby brush past
this moment of light and song
in a rush to get shoes off
and dinner on, just another day
of traffic, bills, and angry bosses.

I stand, mouth open,
holding three lemons,
a pile of sunlight,
          a miracle in yellow,
                    tiny halos

a little girl stops next to me,
giggles, points to the door,
her mother's yank
drags her back to the world of lists.

I fear I will forget
this supermarket vision late tonight,
reaching for the bowl of lemons
and simply seeing fruit.

AMMA'S PRAYER

(for Amma Syncletica)

I belong to that which cannot be seen.
Scorpion's sting, snake's slow hiss,
heat of the stone cave walls,
a portion of bread meant to last for days,
desert draws forth what is essential in me.

I belong to that which cannot be spoken.
I open my parched mouth to sing,
choke on grit and gravel.
Feeling the gray force of the storm rising,
I am stunned into silence.

I belong to that which cannot be heard.
I lie stretched thin across the landscape's aching silence.
Great fields of darkness invite me to rest awhile.
I am borne of bone and breath, flesh and fears,
bitter earth, ground cracked open.

I belong to that which cannot be known.
The sky is burning now, no respite for warriors,
a thousand inner battles under a blazing sun.
Greed, boredom, lust, anger are some of my visitors,
I invite them in for tea scrounged from roots and leaves.

I belong to the One who dwells within.
See, a river of light flows from my lips.
I am she who knows the sun does not rise,
but it is we who stand on the circling earth and
plunge ourselves into that fiery embrace.

ST. FRANCIS AT THE CORNER PUB

Approaching the door, you can already
hear his generous laughter.

He stands on the bar upside down for a moment
to get a new perspective on things,

a flash of polka-dotted boxers
as his brown robe cascades over his head,

sandaled toes wiggling in the air in time with
a fiddle playing in the corner.

Rain falls heavily in the deepening darkness
and he orders a round of drinks

despite his vow of poverty and the single silver coin
in his pocket, multiplied by the last Guinness poured.

Nothing like a good glass of wine, he gleefully says,
heavy Italian accent echoing through the room,

he holds it up to the overhead light, pausing for a moment
lost in its crimson splendor, breathes deeply.

At ease among fishmongers and plumbers,
widows and college students, and the

single mother sneaking out for a moment
of freedom from colic, cries, and diapers.

As the wind blows rain sideways, in come the
animals, *benvenuti* to pigeons, squirrels, seagulls, crows,

and the neighborhood cat balding from mange,
a chorus of yowls, coos, caws, and meows arising,

all huddle around him. No one objects to the growing
menagerie, just glad to be dry and warm.

He clinks glasses all around, no one left out.

LOST PSALM OF KING DAVID

Sitting vigil with the heart's lust,
I am awakened again in the night with
hunger for touch, and moan to know
myself as a stalking, red-eyed lion.

Early steel blue blush brings generous vow
of threshold words. The hour of psalm-writing,
dedicated to the divine and
knowing myself as nightingale.

Late morning I wander to the cypress tree,
where my inner cacophony of voices
concocts murderous plans of victory,
rising like a Leviathan from the sea.

At sun's peak I dance with abandon
in front of the tabernacle. Forgetting
myself for a moment, I become a gathering
of joy and bones on dappled earth.

Green silence of evening presses me
against my someday promise of death,
kindles a warrior's battle grip of anger,
fists held tight like stones, I am steed.

Dandelion seeds float and hover
in the dark like my mind drifting
into dreamscape, full of the majesty
of hawks, and meandering through orchards.

I pluck the apple and see myself
in skin, flesh, seed, stem, and juice dripping.
I know myself as tesserae,
as weightlessness of cloud and heft of rock.

This is all of me, tributaries undulating
out in a hundred directions.
Gather my fragments into Your great hands,
this jumble of caprice and impulses.

We know ourselves as sacred, blessed by the world.
We know ourselves as savage, fighting on too many fine mornings.
I no longer know what to cry out for,
I only know to write this prayer down for all to see.

MIRIAM ON THE SHORES

"All the women went out after her with tambourines and dancing."
—Exodus 15:20

Her skirt hangs heavy with seawater,
staccato breath after running from death.
She can still feel soldiers reaching out
to seize her blouse before the waves caved in.

Collapsing on dry earth for a moment,
the impulse to dance begins in her feet,
spreads slowly upwards like a flock of starlings
rising toward a dawn-lit sky.

So many dances in secret before,
night-stolen movements after exhausting days
heaving stones and harvest.
She finds herself now upright, weeping.

To stand here, face to the sun,
feeling an irrepressible desire to
spin
        tumble
sashay
        turn
shake
        twirl

Savoring freedom with her limbs
as if it were a physical presence
like a fierce wind or the breath of labor,
shackles slipping off slowly.

She couldn't help but dance.
The story says she picked up her tambourine,
which means she had packed it among the essentials.
In fleeing for her life, she knew this would be necessary.

How many of us still live enslaved in Egypt,
beholden and weary?
Do you have the courage to run
across the sea parted just now for you?
Will you carry your musical instrument
and dance right there on the shores?

ST. HILDEGARD STROLLS
THROUGH THE GARDEN

Luminous morning, Hildegard gazes at
the array of blooms, holding in her heart
the young boy with a mysterious rash, the woman

reaching menopause, the newly minted widower,
and the black Abbey cat with digestive issues who wandered
in one night and stayed. New complaints arrive each day.

She gathers bunches of dandelions, their yellow
profusion a welcome sight in the monastery garden,
red clover, nettle, fennel, sprigs of parsley to boil later in wine.

She glances to make sure none of her sisters are
peering around pillars, slips off her worn leather shoes
to relish the freshness between her toes,

face upturned to the rising sun, she sings *lucida materia*,
matrix of light, words to the Virgin, makes a mental
note to return to the scriptorium to write that image down.

When the church bells ring for Lauds, she hesitates just
a moment, knowing her morning praise has already begun,
wanting to linger in this space where the dew still clings.

At the end of her life, she met with a terrible obstinacy,
from the hierarchy came a ban on receiving
bread and wine and her cherished singing.

She now clips a single rose, medicine for a broken heart,
which she will sip slowly in tea, along with her favorite spelt
biscuits, and offers some to the widower

grieving for his own lost beloved,
they smile together softly at this act of holy communion
and the music rising among blades of grass.

GOD AMONG THE POTS AND PANS
(after St. Teresa of Avila)

Sifting flour for daily bread
white mist rises
dough multiplies before my eyes

Chopped carrots
form a broken string
of orange prayer beads

The sharp knife cuts through
any confusion
bone gleaming exposed

Sizzle of steak
onions and mushrooms
alchemy of steel and flame

My cup of coffee
is of course
always a revelation

And the glasses of wine
waiting on the table
a wonder of earth and time

Magpie caws outside
an apparition in black and white
among russet leaves

The sun descends slowly
in violet reverie recalling
the beauty of endings

The timer bell rings
calling me back again
to this prayer

To the miracles
of dinner and dishwater
and our long slow sighs.

ST. TERESA'S ECSTASY

You must have felt it
once or twice yourself
an early winter morning
as the sun tilts slowly
above the earth

bird wings flap fiercely
slicing the sky as it turns
from lavender to blue
your heart a moth
fluttering in a jar

and for a moment you are
so in love with this world
everything is possible
your skin no longer barrier
but portal to communion

like St. Teresa in her moment
of ecstasy, Seraphim with a
golden spear clearing her out
for love, feet bare, head tilted back,
a moan escapes her lips,

rhapsody, relish, swoon
even when the angel recedes
as her tasks call her back
she can still taste bliss in her
pomegranate mouth

and there are glimpses of paradise
even on rain-soaked days
a sun still gleams
among the half-cut lemons,
the egg yolk, my wedding band.

ST. BENEDICT AND THE RAINSTORM

Early February evening.
Benedict and his twin sister Scholastica,
talk for hours about dealing with wayward
monks, childhood memories, regrets, and how they
sometimes steal away to the forest to dance.

The beeswax candle extinguished, she
goes to fetch another, dinner plates
pushed aside with drips of grease left from
roast chicken, celebrating this yearly
time together, the extra jug of wine nearly emptied.

He gets up to leave but she protests.
Benedict's own Rule requires him
to be back at his monastery overnight.
Perhaps she knows she will die only three days later.
Or maybe the rose-hued glimmer of evening astonishes her.

Or this is one of those moments she just wishes
would linger on, her brother's beard shining
silver in the growing moonlight, wanting to
remember the great brown kindness of his eyes,
feeling the rough warmth of his hands in hers.

Her tears rise up,
falling in great splashes,
her weeping calls forth a fierce rainstorm.
Cosmic forces come down on the side of love,
demanding that self-set rules be broken.

I imagine the two of them listening to
the relentless rain beating down around them,
Benedict yielding to the moment, suddenly
seeing the necessity of riverbanks, but also the
widening expanse into the sea.

Perhaps that night they each dreamt that the river
swelled so high it lifted them to the blue bowl of sky,
until the horizon hallowed them.
Until he could see far beyond the stone walls
he had so carefully built.

Perhaps we're here just so that we might say: house,
bridge, fountain, gate, jug, fruit tree, window, —
or finally: column, tower . . . . But to say, I mean,
oh, to speak in such a manner as they could never
have meant them to be in themselves.
    —Rainer Maria Rilke, *The Duino Elegies*

Attention is the beginning of devotion.
    —Mary Oliver

In 2012 my husband and I decided to embark on a life adventure and sold almost everything we owned in Seattle and first moved to Vienna, Austria, the city where my father was from and is now buried. I hold an Austrian passport, so it opened a door to possibility. The poet Rilke became my sustenance during those threshold days of radical unknowing. I loved the way he wrote about the God of darkness and mystery, the God who loves the questions rather than the answers.

After ongoing frustrations with the immigration process for my husband, we headed for Ireland, a place we had fallen in love with on a three-week trip five years earlier. Ireland welcomed us with ease and in Galway, the arts and culture capital, we discovered a vibrant and thriving creative community. For my husband it was theater and film, for myself it was poetry. My poem-writing came alive again in the company of my fellow poets in the Thursday afternoon workshop full of bright, astute, and curious minds. I learned so much about the process of bringing a poem to its essence, playing with what can be released.

The Christian monastic tradition, with roots in desert, Celtic, and Benedictine practice, forms the foundation of my spiritual life. I find much kinship between the way of the monk and the path of the poet. In the Rule of St. Benedict, emphasis is placed on finding the sacred in all things, people, and time. Benedict counsels that the kitchen utensils are as holy as the vessels of the altar. The stranger at the door is to be treated as the very face of Christ. The unfolding of the Hours each day reminds us of the divine dwelling in every moment. This is the call of the monk, but of the poet as well. Both focus on paying attention to life and lifting it up, naming moments, and in the process illuminating their holiness. To see the ordinary anew and to offer that new way of seeing back to the world as gift is the monk's and poet's task.

I read poems to be immersed in the rhythm of their words and the beauty of language. I read them to slow me down, to pause and linger, to freshen my perspective on things. Poetry offers life back to us in language transformed, so our vision is deepened and expanded as well. There is an expansion and enlarging of experience that happens through poetry allowing us to see the spectacle of the ordinary. Poetry reminds us that the utensils of the kitchen are indeed as holy as the chalice, and that life itself is an art.

Poetry has repeatedly saved my life. A line from a poem arrives at the doorway of my imagination and shimmers. Some mornings, in my saner moments, I reach for a book of poems and my journal before turning on my computer or phone and checking mail. Poetry has much in common with dream time, a way of revelation that arrives through an unexpected connection of images.

My own writing arises from a process inspired by the practice of *lectio divina,* or sacred reading. Often a line arrives into my conscious awareness, perhaps from another poem, from a piece of Scripture, or from a conversation, and I sit with it, savor it, allow it to stir and unfold, like a tightly wrapped bud which suddenly breaks open into a bouquet of petals revealing the center of things, and then I listen to its invitation to me. Writing poems often arrives like a dream. I will remember one particular line or image and then gently pull the thread to see where it leads me, how it unfolds.

I write poetry to explore the tension between living in a world of both tremendous beauty and terror. Poetry helps me to rest into this apparent contradiction. In a world filled with terrible news each day, poetry calls me to see the goodness erupting in the dog's exuberant greeting when I come home, in the way that the sun breaks through thick clouds to illuminate a wet field, or the beauty in pausing for a cup of tea. Often writing poems is an overflow of gratitude for moments like these. One of my dearest hopes is those who read these poems will find a moment of sanctuary, a space where they might see the world as enchanted even in the midst of struggle, but never denying the struggle. Poems invite us into an experience outside of time, outside of the relentless linearity of our minds desperate to get on with planning and something productive.

In my book *Eyes of the Heart* I write about photography as a contemplative practice, how it calls us not to "take" photos, but to receive images as gifts. To move from a tight-fisted grasping of the world, to an open-palmed, open-hearted posture of hospitality to what the world freely offers. There is a wonderful Irish story of Kevin and the blackbird, where the saint is described as holding open his palms in prayerful expectation. A blackbird lands there and builds her nest and lays her eggs. The saint is called to an act of loving attention, of not withdrawing from the moment, of staying with discomfort so the new life can emerge. Writing poems is a very similar process to me as photography. I hold my palms open to receive images as gifts. I try not to grasp at the words, but to stay with the discomfort of the creative process until the poem emerges.

Poetry also calls me back to the essence of things. This act of claiming the beauty in simplicity has much in common with the monastic life. I am reminded too, of the ultimate call to that which is essential, the practice of remembering our eventual death. In light of this knowledge, what becomes of the essence? What do I want to leave behind? I know in the moments when I am graced to remember the limitations of my life and the preciousness of my days, what always remains for me is poetry and love. Poetry, for me, is an act of love for the world, a reminder when life feels difficult to love.

Poetry-writing, and not just reading, became central to my spiritual practice again. I am at heart a writer and a soul friend. Even my poems feel like small acts of spiritual direction, pointing to a thousand tiny revelations and reasons for gratitude.

My prayer for you, dear reader, is that you allow life to find you. That you keep your palms open, your heart attuned to love, your spirit leaning into mystery. Consider allowing some time each day to listen to how the world is whispering beneath the rushed and goal-directed surface. To cultivate this kind of attention is to be a poet. We need far fewer how-to manuals and self-help books, and much more poetry.

The following poems had versions previously published in the following books and journals:

"How to Be a Pilgrim," "Please Can I Have a God," "In Praise of Circles," first appeared in *Soul of a Pilgrim: Eight Practices for the Inner Journey*, Ave Maria Press, 2015.

"This is not a poem," "St. Francis and the Corner Pub," "Lost Psalm of King David," "Miriam on the Shores," "St. Brigid and the Fruit Tree," "St. Benedict and the Rainstorm," "St. Hildegard Strolls through the Garden," "Duty of Delight," "Amma's Prayer," "There is No Time for Love to Be Born," and "Whose Silence Are You?" first appeared in *Illuminating the Way: Embracing the Wisdom of Monks and Mystics*, Ave Maria Press, 2016.

"Dreaming of Stones," "Holy Mountain," "St. Gobnait and the Place of Her Resurrection," "St. Ciaran and the Dream," "Flagstone of Loneliness," "St. Colman's Bed," "St. Sourney's Well," "St. Enda Arrives on Inismor," and "St. Brigid and the Fruit Tree" first appeared in *The Soul's Slow Ripening: 12 Celtic Practices for Seeking the Sacred*, Ave Maria Press 2018.

"Compline," "Vigil," "Vespers," and "Lauds" first appeared in *U.S. Catholic* magazine.
"There is No Time for Love to Be Born," is published in *Adam, Eve, & the Riders of the Apolcalypse* (Wipf & Stock).
"Last Night I Dreamt I Was" first appeared on the Galway Review website.
"Holy Mountain" first appeared on the Galway Review website.
"This is How the World is Saved" first appeared in Poetrystuff on the Headstuff website.
"St. Gobnait and the Place of Her Resurrection" first appeared in Poetrystuff on the Headstuff website.
"Wild" first appeared in *Skylight 47* journal.
"Final Instructions" first appeared in *Presence: A Journal of Spiritual Directors International*.
"Dreaming of Stones" first appeared in *Spiritus: A Journal of Christian Spirituality*.
"Inheritance" first appeared in *Skylight 47* journal.
"Flagstone of Loneliness" first appeared in Boyne Berries.
"Listen" first appeared in *Anchor: Where Spirituality and Social Justice Meet*.
"Connemara Illuminated" first appeared in *Tiferet: A Journal of Spiritual Literature*.
"St. Dearbhla's Eyes" first appeared in *Stinging Fly*.
"Cosmos" first appeared *in Tiferet: A Journal of Spiritual Literature*.
"160 East 48th Street" first appeared in *Crannog* journal.
"Sabbath" first appeared in ARTS.
"Tree Dreaming" first appeared in Artis Natura.
"I Want to Know" first appeared in North West Words.
"Thirteen Ways to Love the Rain" first appeared in The Blue Nib.
"God Among the Pots and Pans" appeared first in *Presence: Journal of Catholic Poetry*.
"Pendulum" first appeared in *Presence*: A Journal of Spiritual Directors International.
"Requiem for Myself," "Take My Hand" and "Ripe" appeared on the Eunonia Poetry website.
"Pigeons of Patience" first appeared in *Crannog* journal.

ABOUT PARACLETE PRESS

Who We Are

As the publishing arm of the Community of Jesus, Paraclete Press presents a full expression of Christian belief and practice—from Catholic to Evangelical, from Protestant to Orthodox, reflecting the ecumenical charism of the Community and its dedication to sacred music, the fine arts, and the written word. We publish books, recordings, sheet music, and video/DVDs that nourish the vibrant life of the church and its people.

What We Are Doing

Books

PARACLETE PRESS BOOKS show the richness and depth of what it means to be Christian. While Benedictine spirituality is at the heart of who we are and all that we do, our books reflect the Christian experience across many cultures, time periods, and houses of worship.

We have many series, including *Paraclete Essentials*; *Paraclete Fiction*; *Paraclete Poetry*; *Paraclete Giants*; and for children and adults, *All God's Creatures*, books about animals and faith; and *San Damiano Books*, focusing on Franciscan spirituality. Others include *Voices from the Monastery* (men and women monastics writing about living a spiritual life today), *Active Prayer*, and new for young readers: *The Pope's Cat*. We also specialize in gift books for children on the occasions of Baptism and First Communion, as well as other important times in a child's life, and books that bring creativity and liveliness to any adult spiritual life.

The MOUNT TABOR BOOKS series focuses on the arts and literature as well as liturgical worship and spirituality; it was created in conjunction with the Mount Tabor Ecumenical Centre for Art and Spirituality in Barga, Italy.

Music

The PARACLETE RECORDINGS label represents the internationally acclaimed choir *Gloriæ Dei Cantores*, the *Gloriæ Dei Cantores Schola*, and the other instrumental artists of the *Arts Empowering Life Foundation*.

Paraclete Press is the exclusive North American distributor for the Gregorian chant recordings from St. Peter's Abbey in Solesmes, France. Paraclete also carries all of the Solesmes chant publications for Mass and the Divine Office, as well as their academic research publications.

In addition, PARACLETE PRESS SHEET MUSIC publishes the work of today's finest composers of sacred choral music, annually reviewing over 1,000 works and releasing between 40 and 60 works for both choir and organ.

Video

Our video/DVDs offer spiritual help, healing, and biblical guidance for a broad range of life issues including grief and loss, marriage, forgiveness, facing death, understanding suicide, bullying, addictions, Alzheimer's, and Christian formation.

Learn more about us at our website:
www.paracletepress.com
or phone us toll-free at 1.800.451.5006

 SCAN TO READ MORE

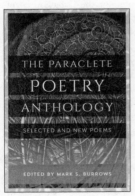